THE F
GROSSEST
JOKE BOOK EVER

Collect them all!

THE FUNNIEST GROSSEST JOKE BOOK EVER

By Joe King

Illustrated by Nigel Baines

First published in 2025 by
Andersen Press Limited
6 Coptic Street, London, WC1A 1NH, UK
Vijverlaan 48, 3062 HL Rotterdam, Nederland
www.andersenpress.co.uk

2 4 6 8 10 9 7 5 3 1

British Library Cataloguing in Publication Data available.

ISBN 978 1 83913 494 4

Printed and bound in Great Britain
by Clays Ltd, Elcograf S.p.A.

Toilet Tomfoolery

**What did one toilet say
to the other toilet?**
'You look flushed!'

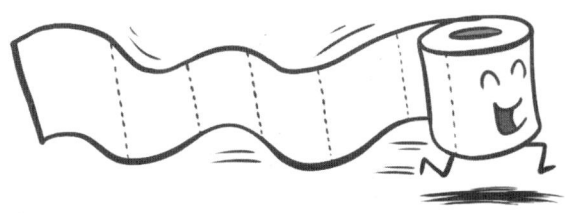

There are two very good reasons why you should never drink toilet water:
Number 1 and number 2

What happens if you miss the toilet while trying to pee?
Urine trouble

Why can't you hear a
Pterodactyl using the toilet?
Because the 'P' is silent

Did you hear the news? The
toilet seats at the local police
station have all been stolen!
It happened two weeks ago,
and the officers have still got
nothing to go on.

**Why were there balloons
in the bathroom?**
There was a birthday potty

**What did one tired piece of
toilet paper say to another?**
'I'm feeling really wiped.'

**Last week, I ran out of toilet
paper and started using old
newspapers instead.
All I can say is that *The Times*
are really rough.**

Why did the volcano explode?
It couldn't find a lava-tory

**Why didn't the toilet paper
make it across the street?**
It got stuck in a crack

**Why did the toilet paper
roll down the hill?**
To get to the bottom

**What should you do if
you find yourself
stuck on the toilet?**
Call in the SQUAT team

**What are toilets
called in heaven?**
Halle-loo-jahs

I bought an ABBA-branded toilet last week.
What a loo

What's the difference between a toilet and a cemetery?
Absolutely nothing – when it's time to go, it's time to go

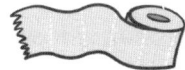

My parents asked me if I could put the toilet seat down. I went in there and shouted: 'You're worthless and no one cares about you!'

Why do Americans leave a penny on the top of the toilet after using it?
So there's always a cent covering the smell

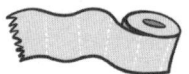

Knock, knock!
Who's there?
Tom Sawyer.
Tom Sawyer who?
Tom Sawyer bum when you were changing your underwear!

What do you see when a duck pulls down his pants?
His butt quack

**Why should you always
take an extra pair of pants
when you go golfing?**
In case you get a hole in one

The best underwear jokes . . .
. . . Are brief

Even my best jokes are pants!

**Why did the priest
need new pants?**
Because they were so hole-y

**Why doesn't Santa
wear any pants?**
Because he's Saint Knicker-less

I'm trying to think of an
underwear joke . . . but I don't
have any clean ones!

I needed some underwear and asked the shop assistant, 'Are these knickers satin?'
'No,' she said. 'They're brand new.'

What does Clark Kent call his bathroom?
The Super Bowl

Why aren't there bathrooms in banks?
Not all banks accept deposits

Did you hear about the woman who ate 10 bowls of alphabet soup?
She's having trouble with her vowels

Why was the accountant with constipation fired?
He just couldn't budget

Student: Do you have holes
in your underpants?
Teacher: Of course not.
Student: Then how do you
get *your feet through?*

**Why did Tigger get
stuck in the toilet?**
He was looking for Pooh

**Why wouldn't the
soldier flush the toilet?**
Because it wasn't his doodie

Knock, knock!
Who's there?
Thumping.
Thumping who?
**Thumping green and slimy
just went up your trousers!**

'Mummy, can I lick the bowl?'
*'No, you have to flush like
everyone else!'*

Knock, knock!
Who's there?
Anita.
Anita who?
Anita go to the bathroom.

Poo Puns

Ready for a poop joke?
No, they stink

What's brown and sticky?
A stick

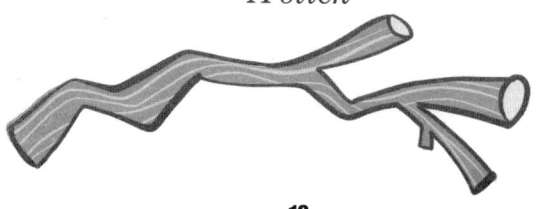

**Poop jokes aren't my
favourite jokes.
But they're a solid number 2.**

**Today I learned that
diarrhoea is hereditary.
It runs in your jeans.**

**Why did the baker
have smelly hands?**
Because he kneaded a poo

**When is the best time to
go to the toilet?**
Poo-thirty

**What's big, brown,
and behind the wall?**
Humpty's Dump

Did you hear about the film Constipated?
It never came out

What do you call a magical poop?
Poodini

'Hello, is this the diarrhoea hotline?'
'Can you hold, please?'

Girl: Every morning at 8 o'clock I have a poo.
Boy: Is that a bad thing?
Girl: Yes, I only wake up at 9.

**Why do most people not like
to talk when poop is around?**
*Because it has a bad
habit of butting in*

Why was the poo sad?
It got dumped

Did you hear about the giant with diarrhoea?
It's all over town

Why did the boy take his own toilet paper to the party?
He was a party pooper

One time I had to pretend I was doing a number 2 in the toilet, so I dropped a bar of soap down it to make a convincing plop . . . It was a sham-poo

How do you know when an octopus has diarrhoea?
It leaves squid marks

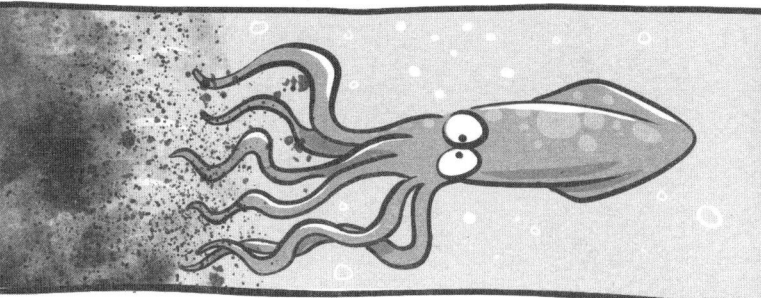

Knock, knock!
Who's there?
I did up.
I did up who?
You did a poo?

Knock, knock!
Who's there?
Smell mop.
Smell mop who?
Gross, no way!

What is a side effect of hilarious poo jokes?

They make your cheeks hurt

What's the difference between the mayor and someone with diarrhoea?

*One runs a city,
the other sits on a runny*

**Poo jokes are hilarious.
Eye jokes are cornea!**

**What happens when a panda
poos in the woods?**
It smells unbearable

**Have you ever noticed that
when you say the word 'poop',
your lips make the same
motion as your bumhole?
Same thing for
explosive diarrhoea!**

**What did the first mate
see in the toilet?**
The captain's log

How does a poo say hello?
'How do you doo-doo?'

Gassy Giggles

I farted at work the other day and my co-worker tried opening the window. It must have been a really bad one – we work on a submarine.

Who are the most dangerous farters in the world?
Ninjas. They're silent but deadly

What do you call someone who refuses to fart in public?
A private toot-er

**What did the poo
say to the fart?**
'You blow me away.'

Did you fart?
*No, that was my bum
blowing you a kiss*

**What's invisible and
smells like worms?**
A bird fart

**What do you get when
a king farts?**
A noble gas

**Did you hear about
the blind skunk?**
He fell in love with a fart

**Success is like a fart . . .
It really bothers others
when it isn't their own.**

**Why shouldn't you
fart in church?**
*Because then you would have
to sit in your pew*

**How can you tell if a
clown has farted?**
Because they will smell funny

How do you know if fart jokes are funny?
They leave you gasping for air

Why is it a bad idea to fart in an Apple store?
Because they don't have Windows

Did you hear about the guy who farted in a lift?
It was wrong on so many levels

Did you hear about the man who farted so much that he died?
His gravestone read 'Let him RIP'

What do you call a Pharoah who rarely farts?
Toot-Uncommon

What can't a spy fart in bed?
Because it would blow their cover

Where do cow farts come from?
Their dairy air

**Why can't a skeleton
fart in public?**
Because he doesn't have the guts

**What's an example of
a big surprise?**
A fart with a lump

**I was suffering with
heartburn, so my friend was
helping me burp at will.
Will did not appreciate it.**

**Why did the grandfather
clock burp every night at 9?**
He just 8!

**What did one burp say
to the other?**
Let's go out the back door

**What happens when
the King burps?**
He issues a royal pardon

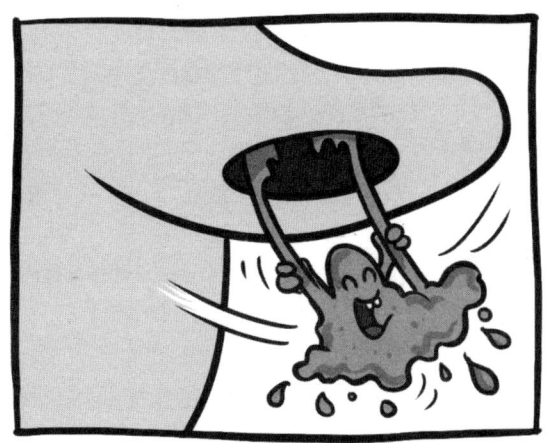

Slimy Squealers

What comes out of
your nose at 150 mph?
A Lamborgreeny

**How do you stop
your nose from running?**
Take away its shoes

**What did the bogey say to the
underside of the desk?**
'I'm stuck on you.'

**What did the bogey write in
its Valentine's Day card?**
'I'd pick you first.'

**What's another word
for a snail?**
A bogey with a helmet

**What do you call a
bogey on a diet?**
Slim Pickings

**Why did the bogey
cross the road?**
Because he was being picked on

**What's the difference between
bogies and broccoli?**
I don't eat broccoli

**Two snowmen decide to have
a cake for dessert.
After taking a bite, one
snowman spits it out and says
it tastes like bogies.
The other snowman says,
'Well, it is carrot cake.'**

Did you pick your nose?
No, I was born with it

What do you do if your nose goes on strike?
Picket

**What happens when
a ghost sneezes?**
Booooooogies go flying

AAACHOOO!

I told my brother his nose is
running. He said, 'It's snot!'

**How do you make
a tissue dance?**
Put some boogey into it

**What do you call someone
who doesn't use a tissue?**
Greensleeves

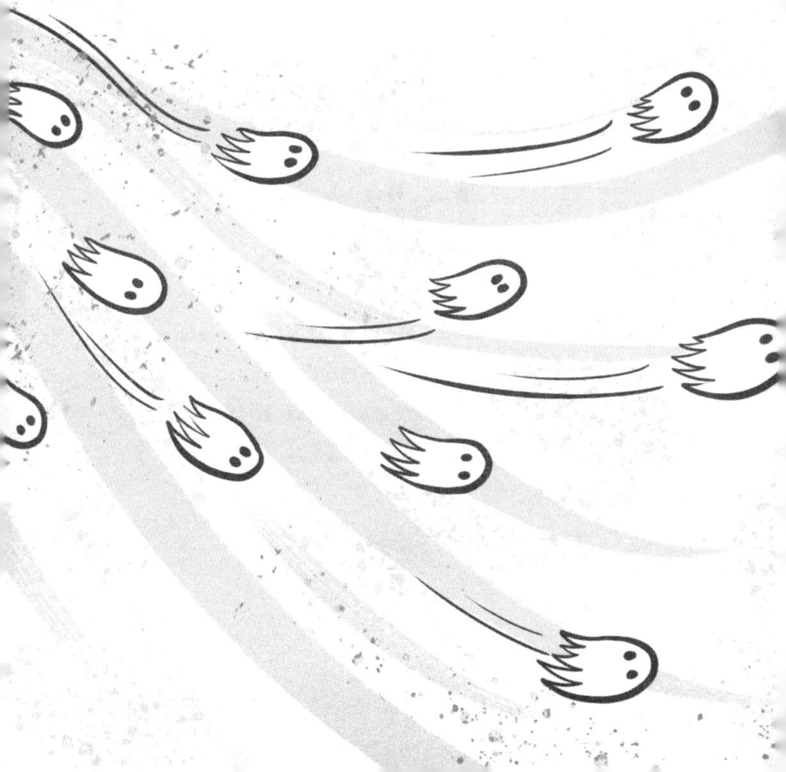

ILL-arious Jokes

What did the elevator say when he sneezed?
'I'm coming down with something.'

**What did the doctor say
to the man who got sick
at the airport?**
'It's a terminal illness.'

**What should you do when
a dinosaur sneezes?**
Get out of the way!

What do you give a sick pig?
Oink-ment

What did one tonsil say to the other?
'Get dressed up, the doctor's taking us out!'

Did you hear the one about the germ? Never mind, I don't want to spread it around.

**Why did the bee go
the doctor?**
Because she had hives

**Where does a boat go
when it's ill?**
The dock

Why don't ants get sick?
*Because they have little anty
bodies*

**Why do surgeons wear masks
in the operating theatre?**
*So that if they make a mistake no
one will know who did it*

I used to work at a hospital, but I got sick of it.

Did you know that dead people can get sick? If you go to the graveyard and put your ear to the ground, you might hear their coffin.

How do you know a person is old?
When they remember the Dead Sea as being just a little sick

Doctor: Did you drink your
medicine after your bath?
*Patient: No, by the time I'd
drunk the bath, there wasn't
room for the medicine!*

Patient: Sometimes I
feel invisible.
Doctor: Who said that?!

Patient: I feel like a window.
Doctor: Where's the pane?

Patient: I keep hearing
a ringing sound.
Doctor: Then answer the phone!

Patient: Doctor, what does this
X-ray of my head show?
Doctor: Unfortunately, nothing.

Patient: My son likes to
pretend he's a small toilet.
Doctor: Maybe he's a little potty.

Patient: Will my measles be
better by next Monday?
*Doctor: I don't want to make
any rash promises.*

Patient: I keep hearing a
buzzing in my ears.
*Doctor: Where did you
expect to hear it?*

Patient: Doctor, have you
taken my temperature?'
Doctor: No, is it missing?

Patient: I keep seeing green aliens
with two heads and four legs.
*Doctor: Have you seen
a psychiatrist?*
Patient: No, just green aliens *with
two heads and four legs.*

Patient: Doctor, I've broken
my arm in two places.
*Doctor: Well don't go back
there again!*

**How did the dentist become
a brain surgeon?**
Her drill slipped

My dentist told me I had
bad breath. I was talking to
someone in the waiting room
at the time.

How do you stop a cold
going to your chest?
Tie a knot in your neck

**Why did the undertaker chop
all his corpses into little bits?**
*Because he liked them to
rest in pieces*

What's Mozart up to now?
Decomposing

**How do you make a
Venetian blind?**
Poke his eyes out

**What do you call a woman
with one leg shorter
than the other?**
Eileen

Did you hear the joke about the body snatchers? I better not say, you might get carried away.

Why did the journalist cut off her fingers?
She wanted to write shorthand

**What do you do if your
kidneys are bad?**
Take them back to the butcher

What's a sick joke?
*Something that comes up
in conversation*

Animal
Howlers

**How do fleas travel
from place to place?**
By itch-hiking

What lies on the ground 100 feet up in the air and smells?
A dead centipede

What has four legs, whiskers, a tail, and flies?
A dead cat

Why do gorillas have big nostrils?
Because they have big fingers

What did the judge say when the skunk walked into the courtroom?
'Odour in the court!'

**What's green and gross
and lives under the sea?**
Shark snot

**What happened to the dog
that ate nothing but garlic?**
His bark was worse than his bite

What did the forgetful skunk say when the wind changed?
'It's all coming back to me now.'

How many skunks does it take to make a big stink?
A phew

Why aren't elephants allowed on the beach?
Their trunks might fall down

What's wet, smelly and goes ba-bump, ba-bump?
A skunk in a tumble dryer

**What do you call a man in a
bathtub full of cowpats?**
An in-cow-poop

**What's the difference between
a maggot and a cockroach?**
*Cockroaches crunch more
when you eat them*

**Which animals didn't go
to the ark in pairs?**
Maggots – they went in apples

**What do you get if you pour
hot water down a rabbit hole?**
Hot cross bunnies

**What goes red, green,
red, green?**
A frog in a blender

What's a lion's favourite food?
Baked beings

What did the slug say when it was thrown over the fence?
'How slime flies!'

What happens when you eat a frog?
You'll croak in no time

What's a lion's favourite food?
Baked beings

(Sickening)
Belly Laughs

**Why is it bad to
upset a cannibal?**
You'll end up in hot water

Thomas finally gave up his dream of being a champion after vomiting at the National Spelling Bee. He'd always be known as an ex-speller now.

What do you call a cannibal who ate his mother's sister?
An aunt eater

First lion: Every time I eat, I feel sick.
Second lion: I know. It's hard to keep a good man down.

Customer: Waiter, why is my apple pie all mashed up?
Waiter: You did ask me to step on it, sir.

Customer: Waiter, there's a dead
beetle in my gravy!
*Waiter: Yes, sir. Beetles are
terrible swimmers.*

Customer: Waiter, there's a
maggot in my soup!
*Waiter: Don't worry, sir, it won't
live long in that stuff.*

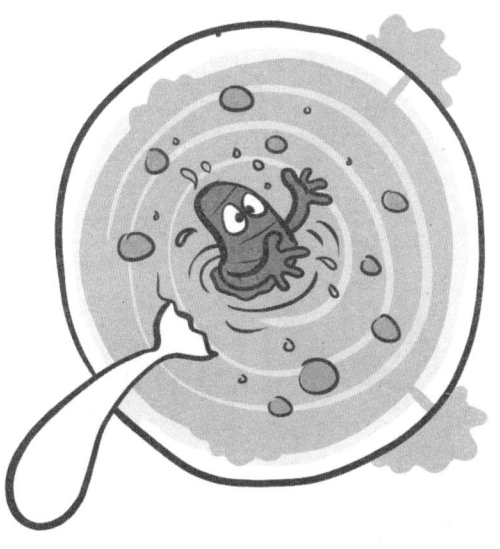

Customer: Waiter, this soup tastes funny.
Waiter: Then why aren't you laughing?

Customer: Waiter, you have your thumbs on my steak!
Waiter: Well, I didn't want to drop it again.

Customer: I'll have the
burger please.
Waiter: With pleasure.
Customer: No, with fries.

Customer: Waiter, is there
any soup on the menu?
Waiter: No, I've wiped it all off.

Customer: Waiter, there's a
spider in my salad.
*Waiter: Good, it must have
eaten the fly.*

Customer: Waiter, there's a
small insect in my soup!
*Waiter: Sorry, sir, I'll get
you a bigger one!*

**What's worse than finding
a worm in your apple?**
*Finding half a worm
in your apple*

**What's green, sticky
and smells like eucalyptus?**
Koala vomit

First cannibal: Your friend
makes a great soup.
*Second cannibal: Yes! But I
am going to miss her . . .*

**What do vegetarian
cannibals eat?**
Swedes

**What do guests do at a
cannibal wedding?**
Toast the bride and groom

**How does Dracula
eat his food?**
In bite-sized pieces

**What is Dracula's favourite
ice cream flavour?**
Vein-illa

**What do frogs order
in a restaurant?**
French flies

**Why was the cannibal
expelled from school?**
*Because he kept buttering
up the teachers*

Rotten Rhymes

A belch is a gust of wind
That cometh from the heart
But should it take a
downward trend,
It turneth to a fart.

*There was a young man
named Bart
Who thought he was
terribly smart.
He ate tons of beans
And busted his jeans
With a loud and
earth-shattering fart.*

Beans, beans, good for your heart:
The more you eat, the more you fart.
The more you fart, the more you eat,
The more you sit on the toilet seat!
Beans, beans, good for your heart:
The more you eat, the more you fart.
The more you fart,
the better you feel,
So let's have beans with every meal

Treacle tart makes you fart,
Custard powder makes it louder,
Apple crumble makes it rumble.

An apple a day keeps
the doctor away.
But an onion a day
keeps everyone away.

*A fart is a musical hum, that
comes from the land of Bum.
It's good for the heart, puts the
body at ease,
Will warm a cold bed and
suffocate the fleas!*

*There once was a young girl
called Fi,
Who desperately needed a wee,
The loo, it was taken,
Left Fi feeling shaken,
So, she ran off in search of a tree!*

There was once a
man from Rangoon
Whose farts could be heard
on the moon.
When you'd least expect 'em
They'd burst from his rectum
With the force of a raging
typhoon.

There was no bigger poo
Once I had that tiramisu.
There was no fruitier fart
Than after eating my tart.
There was no longer wee
Than after twelve cups of tea.
And there was no louder burp
After the coke I did slurp.

Pardon me for being so rude
It was not me, it was my food
It just came up to say 'Hello!'
Now it's gone back down below.

If your bottom burps in public,
Try to say in time:
'Goodness me, what a whiff!
It doesn't smell like mine.'